T175 NETWORKED LIVING
Exploring Information
Communication Techno

Block 3
Entertainment and information
Part 3

Prepared on behalf of the course team
by Chris Bissell, David Chapman, Allan Jones and Geoff Einon

This publication forms part of an Open University course T175 *Networked Living*. Details of this and other Open University courses can be obtained from the Student Registration and Enquiry Service, The Open University, PO Box 197, Milton Keynes MK7 6BJ, United Kingdom: tel. +44 (0)870 333 4340, email general-enquiries@open.ac.uk

Alternatively, you may visit the Open University website at http://www.open.ac.uk where you can learn more about the wide range of courses and packs offered at all levels by The Open University.

To purchase a selection of Open University course materials visit http://www.ouw.co.uk, or contact Open University Worldwide, Michael Young Building, Walton Hall, Milton Keynes MK7 6AA, United Kingdom for a brochure: tel. +44 (0)1908 858785; fax +44 (0)1908 858787; email ouwenq@open.ac.uk

The Open University
Walton Hall, Milton Keynes
MK7 6AA

First published 2005. Second edition 2007.

Edited and designed by The Open University.

Typeset in India by Alden Prepress Services, Chennai.

Printed and bound in the United Kingdom by Halstan Printing Group, Amersham.

ISBN 978 0 7492 1524 8

2.1

COURSE TEAM LIST

Karen Kear, course team chair

Ernie Taylor, course manager

Patricia Telford, course secretary

Academic staff

Mustafa Ali

Chris Bissell

David Chapman

Geoff Einon

Clem Herman

Allan Jones

Roger Jones

John Monk

Nicky Moss

Elaine Thomas

Mirabelle Walker

Judith Williams

John Woodthorpe

Media production staff

Geoff Austin

Deirdre Bethune

Annette Booz

Sophia Braybrooke

Sarah Crompton

Jamie Daniels

Vicky Eves

Alison George

Mark Kesby

Lynn Short

External assessor

Prof. Philip Witting, University of Glamorgan

Contents

Part 3
Computer activities

Chris Bissell, David Chapman, Allan Jones and Geoff Einon

1 Introduction

This part includes computer activities related to both Part 1 and Part 2 of this block. Before starting work, read the study guide in the Block 3 companion. As part of your study planning you should look through the activities and see which are associated with which sections of Parts 1 and 2. You can carry out the computer activities at the time you study the associated text in Part 1 or Part 2, or you can leave the computer activities until later.

2 Spreadsheet basics

If you've never used a spreadsheet before, or are unsure about using one, you should study the material in this section. If you already know how to enter data into a spreadsheet, select and copy/paste cells, and create a column chart, you can test yourself in Activity 4 at the end of the section. Only if you can complete Activity 4 successfully should you move on to Section 3.

The material on spreadsheets in this part of Block 3 gives detailed information for StarOffice, which was supplied to you on the Online Applications CD-ROM. However, if you are already familiar with a different spreadsheet, you may find it preferable to work with the one you are used to. Most spreadsheet programs operate in a similar way, with very similar screen layouts. The biggest differences between spreadsheet programs are in the way that charts are generated. If you already use spreadsheets but are not familiar with producing charts, you may find it easier to use StarOffice, since you will find detailed guidance in this material. Some guidance is given on creating charts in Excel, but if you choose to use Excel, you are expected to be already fairly proficient.

2.1 What is a spreadsheet?

A spreadsheet is a program which allows you to enter, manipulate and display data, including numbers, text, dates and mathematical formulae. It is arranged in a set of columns and rows. In spreadsheets the rows are normally designated by a number and the columns by a letter. This allows you to specify any particular cell in the spreadsheet. For example, the top left cell will be A1. Figure 1 shows a StarOffice spreadsheet, and Figure 2 a Microsoft Excel spreadsheet. In each case cell A1 is selected.

When you start up a spreadsheet, you will be presented with a blank sheet, arranged in rows and columns, similar to those in Figures 1 and 2. You can usually have more than one sheet in a spreadsheet document (called a workbook in some packages), and each sheet can run to many pages if printed out. These sheets can be used to separate out different elements. For example, if you had a spreadsheet document for a company's finances, you might have different sheets to represent different accounts. You can switch between different sheets using the tabs at the bottom of the sheet.

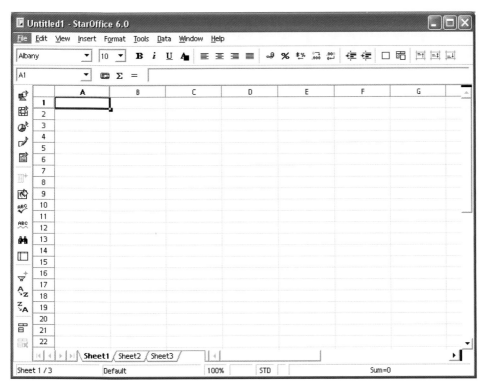

Figure 1   A StarOffice spreadsheet display

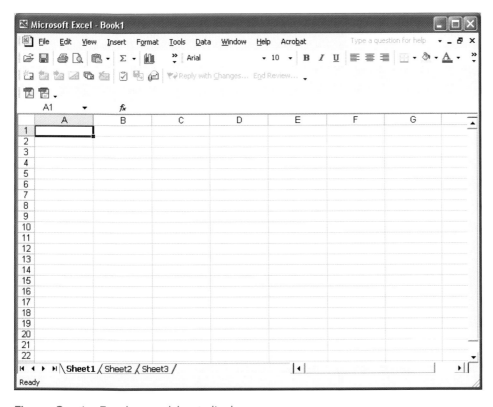

Figure 2   An Excel spreadsheet display

Activity 1 (exploratory)

Look at Figures 1 and 2. What major similarities and differences do you note about the screen displays?

Comment

In many ways the displays are very similar. The general layout of the spreadsheet cells is the same, and each has tabs at the bottom for three separate worksheets. The major difference I noted is in the fine detail of the toolbars, and the fact that StarOffice has a toolbar on the left of the screen as well as at the top. Note, however, that many spreadsheet packages allow you to 'tailor' the toolbars to your own requirements.

Spreadsheets were originally designed for applications in finance and accountancy – in fact, the word 'spreadsheet' originally meant a particular ledger layout used for bookkeeping. The first computer spreadsheets, introduced in the early 1980s, were designed with the aim of automating the sorts of calculation performed by accountants and bookkeepers: totting up columns of figures, for example, calculating interest on loans, or producing quarterly and annual accounts. Spreadsheets rapidly became so popular that they are often referred to as the software 'killer application' that helped popularise the desktop PC. It soon became clear, though, that spreadsheets had many applications outside the world of finance. For example, a spreadsheet allows you to see easily the results of making changes to data you have entered, and to carry out mathematical and other operations on it.

People often talk about spreadsheets enabling you to answer 'What if?' questions. For example, you could have a spreadsheet to examine your consumption of gas and electricity, and the consequences of changing supplier. Or you could set up details of a mortgage and answer questions such as 'What if the interest rate changed to 8%?'.

Spreadsheets consist of cells, into which you can enter data. Some of the most common forms of data are numbers, words and dates. To enter data into a cell, you click on it with your mouse and type the data in. In most spreadsheets the data you are entering will appear in a box called the formula bar, which is below the toolbar. On pressing 'Enter' the cell will now hold the data, and the cell immediately below will be highlighted ready for the next entry.

Suppose, for example, you want to keep your marks from your T175 assignments in a spreadsheet, as shown in Figure 3. You start by selecting the appropriate cell and typing in the data. When you press 'Enter' it is stored in that cell. This 'screenshot' was taken just after I had typed in a score of 69 for my second TMA, but before I pressed 'Enter'.

It is important to realise that the cells you see on the screen are only a small section of the spreadsheet, which can extend far beyond this. The scroll bars are used to move sideways or up and down, as with most modern software. This means you can enter data far beyond the amount you can see on the screen.

Cell contents can be edited by first clicking on the cell and then editing the contents as displayed in the formula bar.

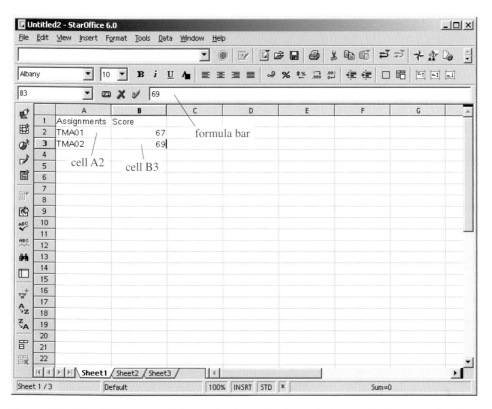

Figure 3   StarOffice spreadsheet display with formula bar, cell A2 and cell B3 indicated

Spreadsheets allow you to specify at the same time a number of cells on which you want to perform an action. If you want to act on a column, you select the letter at the top of the column to highlight the whole column. The same applies to rows, by selecting their numbers. You can also specify a rectangular group (or 'range') of cells by clicking on the first cell, holding down the left mouse button, and dragging across the cells you want in your selection, as shown in Figure 4. You might want to do this in order to copy data from a spreadsheet to paste into a text document, for example.

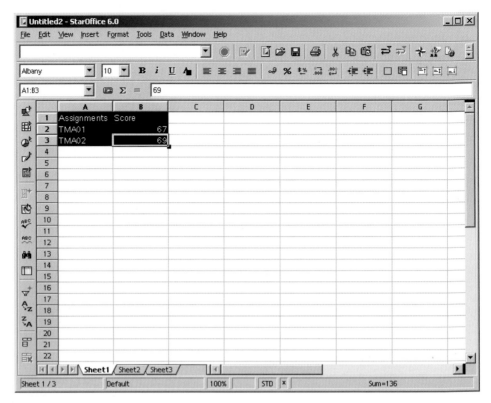

Figure 4 Highlighting a range of cells by clicking and dragging the mouse

Activity 2 (exploratory)

(a) Open up a blank document in your spreadsheet program and create a spreadsheet like that of Figure 3. Then suppose you score 72 in TMA03. Modify your spreadsheet to include this data.

(b) Save your spreadsheet with an appropriate filename. Then select all the data on your spreadsheet (cells A1 to B4 if you've followed my example exactly), copy it to the clipboard (using Edit > Copy or by pressing the 'Control' and 'C' keys together), and minimise the spreadsheet window. Now open up a word-processing document, and paste the contents of the clipboard into your word-processing document. If you are using StarOffice select Edit > Paste Special and Formatted Text. If you are using Microsoft Word just select Edit > Paste or press 'Control' and 'V' together.

Comment

The modified data should automatically appear in your word-processing document as a table, something like this:

Assignments	Score
TMA01	67
TMA02	69
TMA03	72

Most spreadsheet and word-processing software allows various copy and paste options, including pasting the spreadsheet selection as a 'mini-spreadsheet' or a graphics object. So don't worry if you get something unexpected as a result of this activity. It will depend not only on which software packages you are using, but on how the software preferences are set up.

As new versions of spreadsheet programs were marketed, more and more facilities were added for display, calculation, and mathematical functions. This means that current spreadsheets are very powerful, but can be quite confusing. One of the aims of this part of Block 3 is to enable you to use just a few of the myriad possibilities of spreadsheets with confidence.

2.2   Creating a spreadsheet with a column chart

Now you will enter data into a spreadsheet and use it to generate a column chart.

Activity 3 (exploratory)

The following table gives some information about the growth of the internet over the period from 1996 to 2002. Open up your spreadsheet package and enter the data in columns A and B. Save the file with a suitable name (and back it up!) – you will need it later.

Year	Millions of internet hosts
1996	9.47
1997	16.15
1998	29.67
1999	43.23
2000	72.40
2001	109.57
2002	147.34

In StarOffice you should see something very like Figure 5.

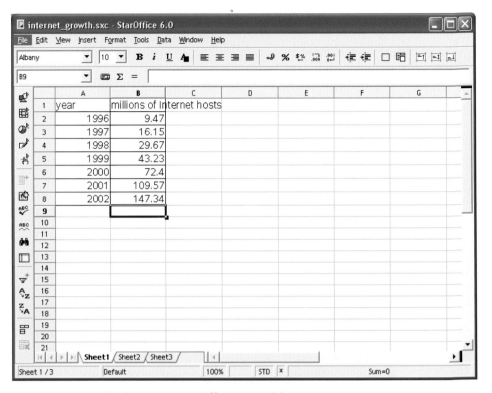

Figure 5   Sample data in a StarOffice spreadsheet

Now select (by highlighting them) the numerical values you want to plot (cells A2 to B8) and then choose Insert > Chart from the menu. You will see the 'Autoformat Chart' dialogue box asking you to choose a column or a row as 'Label'. In order to label the horizontal axis of your chart with the years listed in column A, check 'First column as label', as shown in Figure 6.

A few clicks on the 'Next' button will enable you to accept the default settings for chart type and chart variant, which are the ones we want to use here, and should take you through the creation of a column chart. When you see the box subtitled 'display', complete it as shown in Figure 7, to provide:

1   a title for your chart

2   a title for the horizontal axis (x-axis)

3   a title for the vertical axis (y-axis).

If you want to know what the 'Legend' box does, just experiment later! For now, make sure it is unchecked.

When you are happy with your entries in this box, click 'Create'.

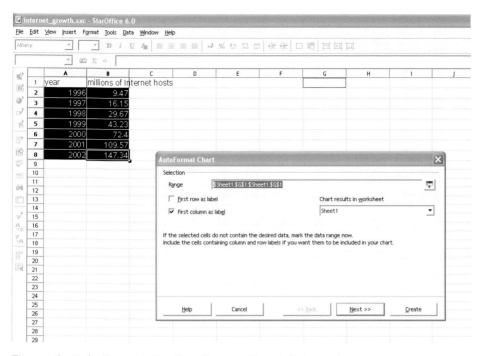

Figure 6 Labelling via the 'AutoFormat Chart' dialogue box

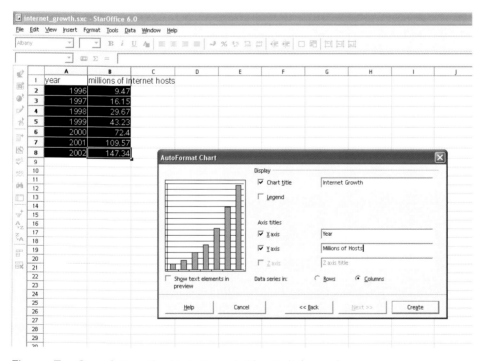

Figure 7 Completing the 'AutoFormat Chart' dialogue box

Comment

You should now have a display looking like Figure 8.

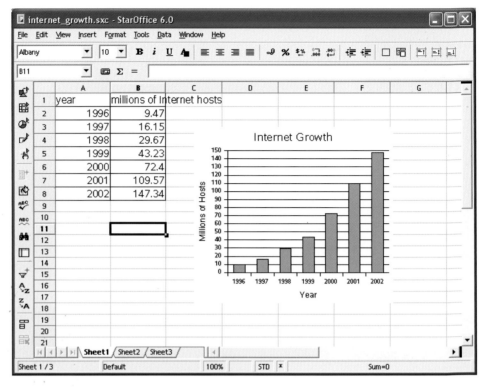

Figure 8 Chart created from a spreadsheet

Save the file with a suitable filename.

Activity 4 (self-assessment)

The following table gives data about the growth of mobile telephony in the USA.

Year	Millions of US mobile phone subscribers
1989	2.69
1990	4.37
1991	6.38
1992	8.89
1993	13.07
1994	19.28
1995	28.15
1996	38.2

Use your spreadsheet software to produce a column chart of this growth. If you make a mistake and need to change anything, remember that cell contents can be modified by first clicking on the cell and then editing the contents as displayed in the formula bar. Save your spreadsheet for later.

Comment

My answer is given at the end of this part.

What if I'm using Excel?

The procedure using Excel is similar, but the details differ.

Enter the data in columns A and B as before, but to create the chart, select only the data in cells B2 to B8. Then click on the chart wizard icon on the toolbar (or use Insert > Chart) and use 'Next' to go through the process.

Step 1: Accept the default settings you are offered.

Step 2: Accept default settings on 'Data Range' tab.

On the 'Series' tab select 'Category (X) axis labels' and highlight cells A1 to A8. Your display should look like Figure 9.

Step 3: Add titles for the chart and the two axes as for StarOffice in Figure 7 above.

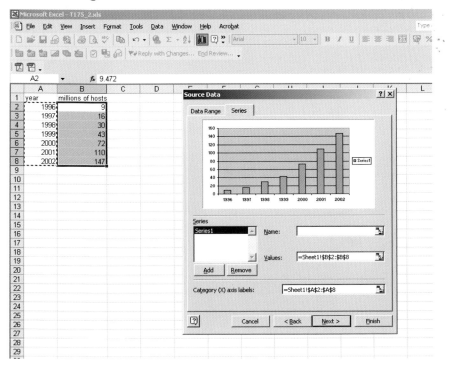

Figure 9 Excel chart source data dialogue box

3 Spreadsheet activities for Parts 1 and 2

In this section you will carry out a number of activities associated directly with other parts of Block 3. The practical work in Sections 3.1 and 3.2 is linked to Part 1, while that in 3.3 and 3.4 is linked to Part 2.

3.1 Using formulae

So far you've simply entered numerical data into a spreadsheet directly. But the most important feature of spreadsheets is that they can perform all sorts of computations and mathematical operations for you. So now you'll use a spreadsheet to investigate how the number of different binary words varies with the word length. We began to look at this in Part 1 of this block, but the spreadsheet allows us to look easily at longer word lengths and also to investigate the nature of the relationship between the word length and number of different words which can be represented.

To start with, we'll look at words with lengths from 1 to 8 bits. But instead of entering the values 1 to 8 in the spreadsheet manually, we'll use a formula which will allow us to enter the values automatically.

Open a new spreadsheet document and enter 1 in cell A1. To use a formula to produce the rest of the values needed in column A, type:

$= A1 + 1$

into cell A2. The '=' sign indicates that the spreadsheet program will treat the cell contents as a formula, rather than a number, or text. Press 'Enter' and then select cell A2 again. You should see the screen shown as Figure 10.

Note that the formula bar shows the formula that you entered ($= A1 + 1$), but the cell shows the value that results from calculating the formula. That is, the cell shows the result of adding 1 to the value in A1, giving the value 2. Now, the power of spreadsheets lies in the way such formulae can be copied. Select cell A2 again, and copy/paste it into cells A3 to A8 (you can do this by first selecting A2, then 'Copy', then select all of A3 to A8, then 'Paste'). Look at the values in the cells, and the formula in each cell (by selecting the individual cell and examining the formula bar). When copied down, the spreadsheet has interpreted the formula '$= A1 + 1$' as 'the value in this cell is one more than the value in the cell above' (Figure 11).

Now, we're going to use this facility to calculate the number of possible values associated with a binary word of a given length. Select (highlight) row 1 by clicking on the '1' at the left of the first row. Then use the

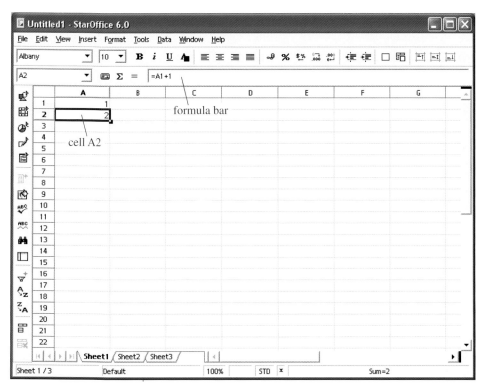

Figure 10   StarOffice spreadsheet display with formula bar and cell A2 indicated

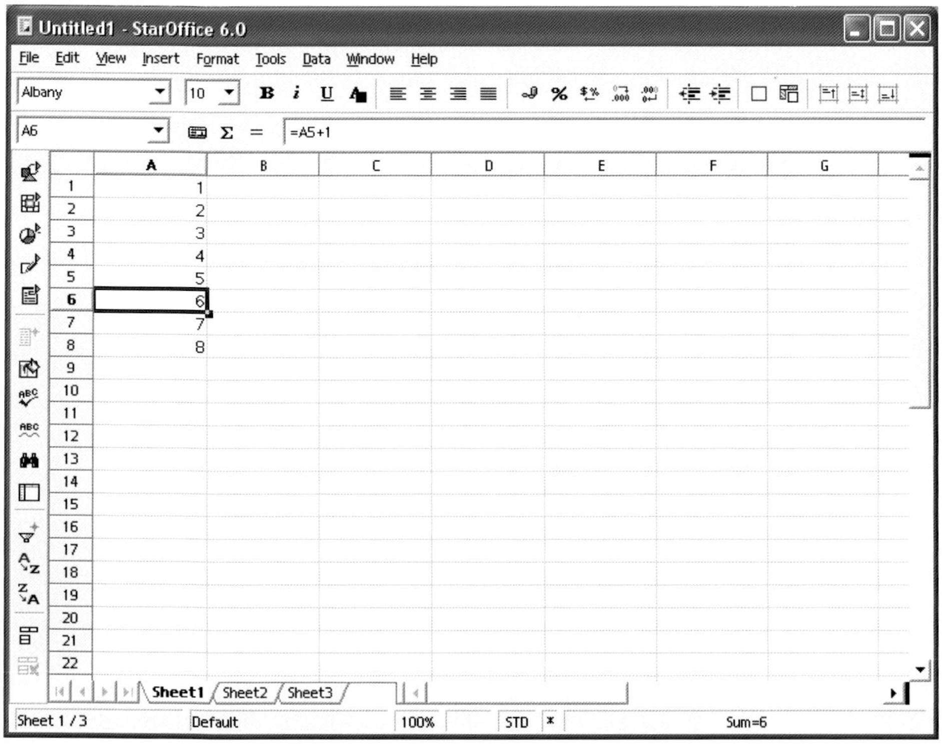

Figure 11   Spreadsheet display with values in cells A3 to A8

Insert > Row command to create a new row at the top. Type in some titles for the columns.

A 1-bit word has two possible values (just binary 1 or binary 0), so enter 2 in cell B2. Your spreadsheet should look like Figure 12. Save the file.

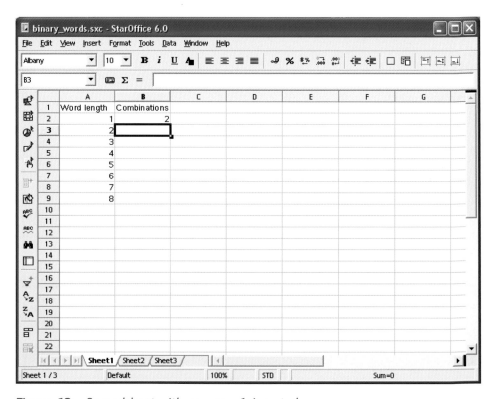

Figure 12 Spreadsheet with new row 1 inserted

Activity 5 (exploratory)

Click on one or two of the cells A2 to A9 and see, from the formula bar, how the formulae have been affected by inserting the new row 1.

Comment

The spreadsheet has automatically 'updated' the cell references to take into account the fact that they've all been shifted down by one.

Activity 6 (exploratory)

In column A we copied a formula so as to increase the value of each cell by 1. I hope you remember from your study of this block that increasing the length of a binary word by 1 bit doubles the number of values that can be represented. Can you suggest a formula for cell B3 that will double the value of the cell above? Hint: the symbol * is used for multiplication instead of × in most computer applications.

Comment

The formula is '=B2*2'.

Enter this formula in cell B3 and copy it down. You should see something like Figure 13.

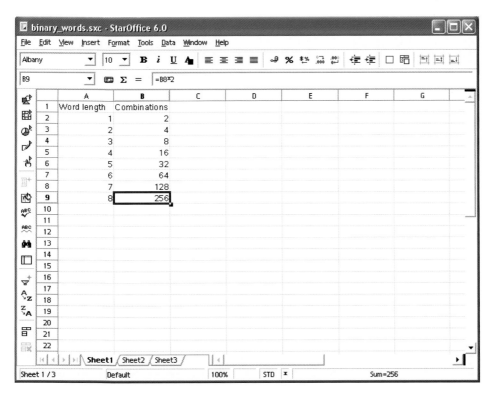

Figure 13 Spreadsheet with values in cells B3 to B9

The spreadsheet has interpreted the formula as 'this cell is double the value of the cell above'.

Finally, create a column chart, with suitable labels, from your spreadsheet as shown in Figure 14.

3.2 Dealing with large ranges of numbers

Now you will extend your previous spreadsheet to word lengths up to 16 bits.

First, delete the chart by clicking on it and pressing 'Delete'. Then simply copy the formulae in the cells of each column down to 16 bits, select the appropriate cells, and create a new chart. Resize the chart if you need to. You should obtain something like Figure 15.

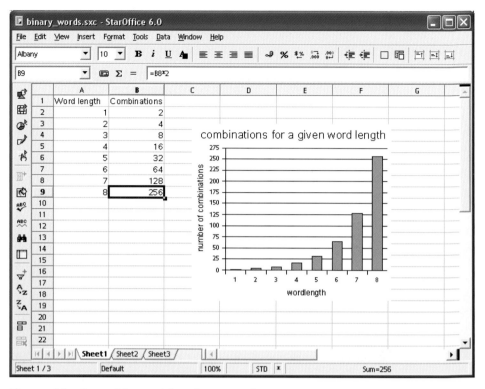

Figure 14 Spreadsheet with column graph

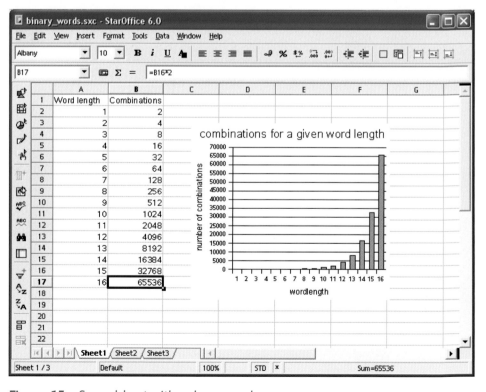

Figure 15 Spreadsheet with column graph

Activity 7 (exploratory)

If you were given this chart, without the numbers in columns A and B, and asked to say something about word lengths from 1 to 6, what would be your response?

Comment

On the face of it, it looks as though they might all be zero. But as it stands, it's just impossible to say. The range of the vertical (y) axis doesn't allow any detail until you get above a 10-bit word length.

In order to cope with situations such as this, a different sort of plot is often used. Instead of a vertical (y) axis with a linear scale, a logarithmic scale is used.

On a **linear scale**, each increment on the scale corresponds to adding a certain amount. So, in Figure 15 the scale is labelled in increments of 5000: 0, 5000, 10 000, 15 000, ... – we add 5000 each time.

linear scale

On a **logarithmic scale**, each increment on the scale corresponds to multiplying by a certain amount. So, a logarithmic scale might be labelled 1, 10, 100, 1000, ... – multiplying by 10 each time.

logarithmic scale

On your spreadsheet, double-click on the chart (in StarOffice you should get a grey border), then double-click on the vertical axis and check the 'logarithmic' box for the 'y-axis scale'. Click on 'OK' and you should see a window similar to that shown in Figure 16. Save the document with a new filename.

(In Excel it's very similar: double-click on the vertical axis, then check the 'logarithmic' box under the 'Scale' tab.)

Activity 8 (exploratory)

Have a good look at Figure 16.

(a) Which feature strikes you immediately?

(b) Now look at the values of the data in the spreadsheet columns. Can you easily associate the number of different values with the heights of the columns? Try a 10-bit word first and then one or two other word lengths.

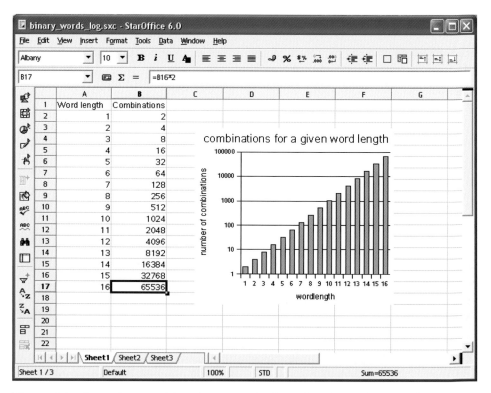

Figure 16 Spreadsheet with column graph plotted on logarithmic scale

Comment

(a) The most striking feature is that with the logarithmic scale the heights of the columns form a straight line. You can now see more detail of the smaller word lengths.

(b) From the chart we see that the 10-bit word corresponds to about 1000 combinations – pretty close to the actual value of 1024. But it is not easy to estimate the values associated with heights of columns that fall between the main gridlines, although it is possible to do this with practice (see box). In many logarithmic plots, intermediate grid lines are included; not all spreadsheets offer this option, however, and the details are not important here.

Logarithmic (log) plots such as this are useful for displaying charts with a very large range of values, and you will see them used in various circumstances.

Interpreting logarithmic scales

To interpret logarithmic scales approximately by eye, you have to remember the defining feature of such a scale – that is, moving the same distance up the scale corresponds to multiplying by a given factor. So, for example, about halfway between 1 and 10 on a logarithmic scale corresponds to multiplying by a factor of just over 3. This is because $1 \times 3 = 3$, and $3 \times 3 = 9$, just below 10.

Looking again at Figure 16, we see that the column height (32) for a 5-bit word falls almost exactly halfway between 10 and 100 on the logarithmic scale. If we multiply 10 by 3.2 we get 32; if we multiply 32 by 3.2 we get 102.4 – very close to 100.

In this example, the number of possible values increases in a very particular way as the word length increases: it doubles for each increase in word length of 1 bit. Growth like this is called exponential. Any growth where the value increases by a given factor with respect to something else is exponential – for example, compound interest on a savings account is an example of exponential growth with respect to time. The term is often misused, however. You will hear people refer to any rapid growth as 'exponential'.

Plotting data using a logarithmic scale offers a rough-and-ready way of checking whether growth really is exponential – if it is, the column heights will form a straight line.

Activity 9 (self-assessment)

The area of a square is given by the length of a side multiplied by itself – this is the origin of the mathematical term 'the square of a number'. Set up a spreadsheet to calculate the areas of squares with sides 5, 10, 15, ... , 100. (Remember that you can fill in these numbers automatically using an appropriate formula.)

Note that you can also use a formula to calculate the square of a number. If the length of the side is held in cell A2, for example, a formula giving the area is:

    = A2*A2.

Is this type of growth exponential?

Comment

The answer is given at the end of this part.

Activity 10 (self-assessment)

Now check whether the data on (i) the growth of the internet (from Activity 3) and (ii) the uptake of mobile phones (from Activity 4) is exponential.

Comment

My answer is given at the end of this part.

3.3   The grapevine

You are probably familiar with how fast news can travel via the 'grapevine'. You tell a story to a couple of people who each tell it to two or three more people and so on. Before you know it, everyone has heard the story. We can easily model the spread of news in this way if we make some simplifying assumptions. (Modelling always involves simplifications.)

1   Assume the story is passed on in orderly fashion, with 'generations' in the spread. The first generation is when you tell other people. The second generation is when they tell people, the third when the people they have told tell other people and so on.

2   Assume that each person tells the same number of people. Thus, if you tell two other people, they also each tell two people.

3   Assume everyone tells someone new, who has not heard the story before.

Activity 11 (exploratory)

Make a spreadsheet that tabulates the number of people who are told the story in each generation for the two cases of each person telling just two other (new) people and each person telling just three other (new) people. Display the results on a bar chart, and decide whether the growth in the number of people being told the story is exponential.

I suggest you list the generations in column A as 1, 2, 3, 4, ... , and put the number of people being told the story in columns B and C (use B for when two people are told each time and column C for when three people are told each time. Take your data up to 15 generations – in other words, column A holds the numbers 1 to 15.

After the first few rows with headings and the first data you will be able to use formulae that you copy and paste to get the rest of the table. See if you can work out what formulae to use for yourself, before looking at my answer.

Comment

My spreadsheet is shown in Figure 17. In column A I just counted up using the same formula that we used in the last activity, so that cell A4 contains ' = A3 + 1' and I then copied this into the cells below far enough to get to generation number 15. In B3 I put the number 2 and in C3 the number 3 for the number of people told in the first generation.

In column B, the number of people told increases in each generation by a factor of two, so in cell B4 I put the formula:

$$= B3*2$$

and copied this down to B17. Likewise for column C the increase is a factor of 3 in each generation, so I put:

$$= C3*3$$

in cell C4 and copied this to all cells down to cell C17.

I then selected cells in the range A2 to C17 and inserted a chart. After inserting the chart I changed the vertical axis to a log scale. You can see from Figure 17 that for both 'two per generation' and 'three per generation' the increase on the log scale looks like a straight line, indicating that in both cases the increase is exponential.

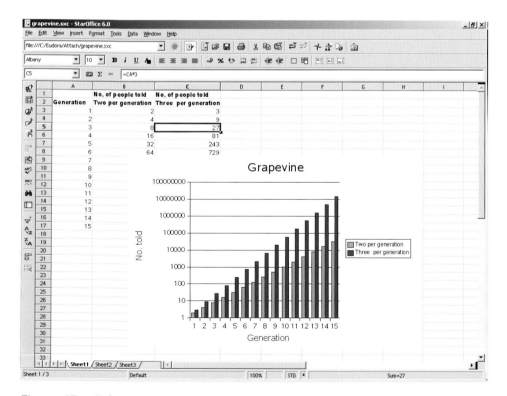

Figure 17 Column graph with two sets of data plotted

3.4 The price of flash memory

Taylor, in his updating paper for Part 2 of this block (Taylor, 2004), says:

> [T]he cost per gigabyte of flash memory is reducing by a factor of around 4 per annum.

I checked on the internet in April 2005 and found that four gigabytes of flash memory cost about £250.

Activity 12 (exploratory)

Use a spreadsheet to tabulate the expected cost of four gigabytes of flash memory each year for the ten years from 2005 to 2014. Assume that (a) each year the cost is a quarter of what it was the year before, and (b) this rate of cost reduction remains steady over the period.

In order to display small numbers you might need to change the cell number format. To do this in StarOffice, you highlight the cells you want to change then select 'Cells' from the 'Format' dropdown menu. You then select the 'Numbers' tab. I suggest you work with numbers to 4 decimal places and 1 leading zero (i.e. a single zero before the decimal place). This is shown in Figure 18.

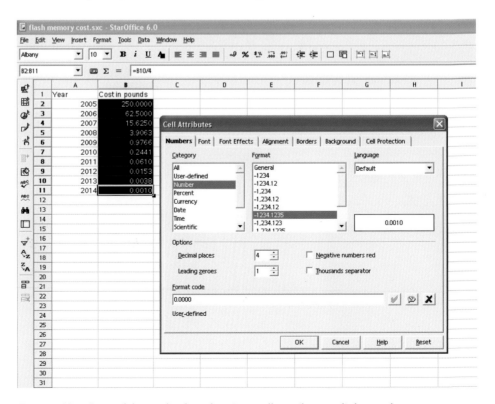

Figure 18 Spreadsheet display showing cell attributes dialogue box

Generate a chart of the costs each year with a log scale for the vertical axis.

How accurate do you think this model will be? How much does it predict that 4 gigabytes of flash memory will cost in 2008? And in 2014?

Comment

My answer is shown in Figure 19.

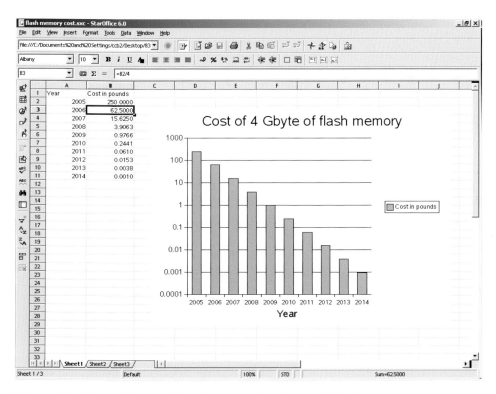

Figure 19   Spreadsheet with column graph of cost of flash memory

Notice how the plot on a log scale is again linear, but that it is falling. This is an example of exponential decay. Just as multiplying repeatedly by a given factor results in exponential growth, so dividing repeatedly by a factor (dividing by 4 each year in this case) causes exponential decay.

The model predicts the cost of 4 gigabytes of flash memory to be about £4 in 2008, and £0.001 or 0.1p in 2014. A cost of £4 in 2008 might be correct, although I suspect that you would not be buying memory in that sort of quantity. Maybe the smallest size you'll be able to buy will be 25 gigabytes for £25. A price of 0.1p for 4 gigabytes in

2014 sounds improbable to me, and I do not think that the price will continue falling at the same rate up until then.

However, it is true to say that over the last few decades we've seen remarkably consistent exponential growth of memory size and computing power per unit cost. This is known as Moore's Law, after the person who first spotted the trend. How long it can continue is anyone's guess.

4 Graphics

4.1 Introduction

In this section we shall be putting into practice some of the ideas you have already met about pixels, file sizes and data compression. You will be using your computer in a series of activities that are introduced and discussed below.

The following activities use a graphics editing package called IrfanView. This was installed from the course DVD with the T175 Guide. You launch IrfanView from either the desktop icon or your Windows Program menu. You will use IrfanView to look at and modify some graphics files. These files were installed in C:\T175\Block_3_Images when you installed the T175 Guide, unless you chose to install them to a different folder. If you chose to install them to a different folder, they will be in C:\MyPath\T175\Block_3_Images, where 'MyPath' is the path you used during installation. As you will be working on these files you might like to take backup copies before you begin.

If you have a digital camera you probably already have something similar to IrfanView on your computer. However, I advise you to use IrfanView rather than your own graphics editing application unless you are already quite experienced with computer graphics. IrfanView is quite a small application and will not encroach greatly on your hard-disk space.

You will also be using the *T175 Colour demonstrator*, which you launch from the T175 Guide.

For the following activities you need to be sure that your computer is set up to show filename extensions. These are the three- or four-letter codes that are automatically added to filenames. If you are used to seeing such things as .doc, .xls, .jpg, .mp3 and so on at the ends of filenames, then your computer is showing extensions. If you are not used to seeing these, then you need to turn them on. The usual way to do this is to go to My Computer, and find Folder Options (under 'Tools' in Windows ME, 2000 and XP, or under 'View' in Windows 98). In Folder Options, select the 'View' tab. Remove the tick from 'Hide extensions from files of known type' (Figure 20). Click on 'Apply to all folders' or 'like current folder'.

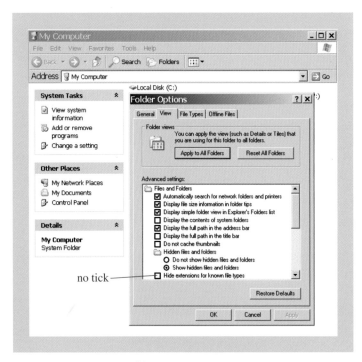

Figure 20 Showing filename extensions

4.2 Greyscale

Look at the two sketches in Figures 21 and 22. These are by the same artist, E. Allan Jones (1919–2000), and show scenes near Stockport, England.

Figure 21 *Reddish Vale*

Figure 22 *Mellor*

In terms of their size on the page, these two pictures are virtually the same, as you can see.

You can find files of each of these pictures in the folder Block_3_Images (see my note in Section 4.1 about the location of this folder). They are Reddish Vale.bmp and Mellor.bmp. Use IrfanView to open 'Mellor.bmp' (use File > Open ...). Possibly a portion of the picture will fill your screen. If so, you need to zoom out a few times, which you can do by pressing the minus sign on your keyboard or by pressing the 'Zoom out' button (see Figure 23).

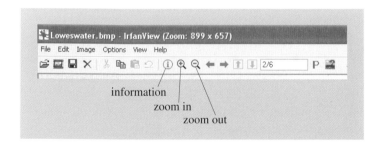

Figure 23 IrfanView

With Mellor.bmp open, press the 'Information' button (see Figure 23). You will see something like Figure 24.

There are several points to notice here. Resolution is 150 dots per inch (DPI) both horizontally and vertically. In this context a 'dot' is a pixel.

If you look at 'Current size' (seventh line down), you can see that 'size' here means 'number of pixels', which in this case is just over 2 million

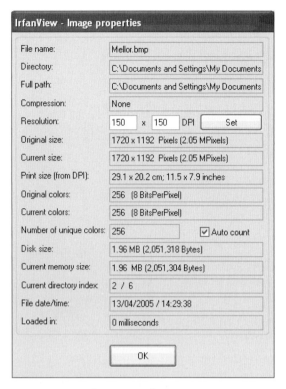

IrfanView - Image properties	
File name:	Mellor.bmp
Directory:	C:\Documents and Settings\My Documents
Full path:	C:\Documents and Settings\My Documents
Compression:	None
Resolution:	150 x 150 DPI Set
Original size:	1720 x 1192 Pixels (2.05 MPixels)
Current size:	1720 x 1192 Pixels (2.05 MPixels)
Print size (from DPI):	29.1 x 20.2 cm; 11.5 x 7.9 inches
Original colors:	256 (8 BitsPerPixel)
Current colors:	256 (8 BitsPerPixel)
Number of unique colors:	256 ☑ Auto count
Disk size:	1.96 MB (2,051,318 Bytes)
Current memory size:	1.96 MB (2,051,304 Bytes)
Current directory index:	2 / 6
File date/time:	13/04/2005 / 14:29:38
Loaded in:	0 milliseconds

OK

Figure 24   IrfanView information pane

pixels (2.05 Mpixels). The information pane distinguishes between 'Original size' and 'Current size' because you can make the picture bigger or smaller if you wish to. (I will not be discussing this.)

In 'Current colors', the information pane shows there are 256 colours. Again there is a distinction between original and current values because you can adjust the number. For the moment, leave it at 256.

The term 'colour' is unfortunately used ambiguously and inconsistently in this context. Both *Mellor* and *Reddish Vale* could be described as 'monochrome', which literally means 'one colour'. By implication that one colour is black. (White is assumed to be present as well.) This description does not fit *Mellor* particularly well because there are many shades of grey. Another term that could be used for both pictures is 'greyscale', meaning that they consist only of shades of grey, although this description does not fit *Reddish Vale* particularly well. In everyday speech we would say that neither picture had colour, because we think of colour as being missing from black-and-white or monochrome images. However, in the context of Figure 24, 'colour' includes shades of grey as well as the everyday sense of colour.

Figure 24 shows that 8 bits per pixel are used to represent 'colour'. Eight bits correspond to 256 different values ($256 = 2^8$). In this context, then, a 'colour' is any one of those 256 different numbers. So, for instance, the binary number 0000 0001 is one colour, and 0000 0010 is another.

Both 'Original colors' and 'Current colors' tell you the maximum number of different colours you can have when you use (in this case) 8 bits per pixel. However, this is not necessarily the same as the number of colours present in the picture: the picture might actually have fewer colours. For instance, the picture might not have any pure white regions. The 'Number of unique colors' in the information pane tells you how many colours there are, rather than how many there could be. In this case, the number of colours used is the maximum possible: 256.

The last points in the information pane that I want to discuss are 'Disk size' and 'Current memory size'.

'Disk size' refers to the size of this file on your hard drive. As you can see from the figure in brackets, it is 2 051 318 bytes. This is not surprising, as the picture has 2.05 million pixels (from the 'Original size' part), and each pixel is represented by 8 bits, or 1 byte. So 2.05 million bytes of data are needed to represent the picture. You might wonder why this is expressed in Figure 24 as 1.96 MB, rather than 2.05 MB. It is because the 'M' here represents not 1 000 000 but 1 048 576, or 2^{20}. When you take that into account, the answer comes out at a number very close to 1.96 MB.

'Current memory size' refers to the amount of space taken by this picture in your computer's RAM. It is important to appreciate that when a file is open on your computer, as Mellor.bmp is, the file exists in two places. It is on the hard drive and in the computer's RAM. If you edit the open file, you edit the version in the RAM, but the stored version on the hard drive is unchanged until you perform a Save command.

In Figure 24, 'Current memory size' (the size of the file in RAM) is practically the same as 'Disk size' (the size of the file on the hard drive). For a file such as this, where no compression is used, this is usual. However, if, for example, the file had been supplied as a JPEG file, rather than a BMP file, the 'Disk size' would have been less than the 'Current memory size'. Loading a compressed file into RAM involves a decompression process.

Activity 13 (exploratory)

Open the file Reddish Vale.bmp and look at the information pane. How does it compare with that for Mellor.bmp? Unfortunately IrfanView does not allow you to have more than one picture open at a time, so you cannot see both information panes at the same time. However, if you enter the data for *Reddish Vale* in Table 1, you should be able to compare the two pictures quite easily. (In Table 1 I have omitted irrelevant image properties.)

Table 1 Data for *Mellor* and *Reddish Vale*

Image property	Mellor	Reddish Vale
Resolution	150 × 150 DPI	
Original size	1720 × 1192 pixels (2.05 Mpixels)	
Current size	1720 × 1192 pixels (2.05 Mpixels)	
Print size	29.1 × 20.2 cm, 11.5 × 7.9 inches	
Original colors	256 (8 bits per pixel)	
Current colors	256 (8 bits per pixel)	
Number of unique colors	256	
Disk size	1.96 MB (2 051 318 bytes)	
Current memory size	1.96 MB (2 051 304 bytes)	

Comment

You should have found that the data for Reddish Vale.bmp was very similar to that of Mellor.bmp, except in one respect. In Reddish Vale.bmp the number of unique colours is 2, whereas in Mellor.bmp it is 256.

The difference revealed in the last activity is not too surprising if you compare the two pictures visually. *Mellor* is a pencil sketch, and the artist has used varying degrees of pressure on the pencil to vary the shade of grey. In fact, the original picture would not have had any set number of colours. By varying the pressure on the pencil appropriately, an infinite number of shades of grey can be created. In other words, there is no fixed set of greyness values in the original picture – although there are maximum and minimum values, corresponding to black and white. This scope for unlimited variation between the maximum and minimum values is characteristic of analogue representation. The process of scanning the picture to create a digital graphics file has limited the number of levels of grey to, in this case, 256. Greys in the original picture that do not correspond exactly to any of the 256 available levels are represented, during digitisation, by the nearest level. Digitisation therefore imposes a scale of allowed values. If more than 8 bits per pixel had been used, the scale of allowed values would have been more finely graded. (If you like, the rungs of the ladder would have been closer together.) Unlike the *Mellor* picture, *Reddish Vale* is a pen-and-ink sketch. In pen-and-ink there is no possibility for creating shades of grey. Each part of the picture is either black or white. This is why the 'Number of unique colors' for Reddish Vale.bmp is two.

Colour depth is the term used to represent the maximum number of possible colours in a digital image. We can express colour depth either as a number of levels or as a number of bits per pixel. So, for instance we would speak of a colour depth as 256 colours, or as 8 bits per pixel (or just '8 bits').

4.3 Reducing the file size

In Reddish Vale.bmp, using 8 bits per pixel is extravagant, because only two of the 256 possible values of 'greyness' are used.

Activity 14 (self-assessment)

(a) What is the smallest number of bits per pixel that can be used in Reddish Vale.bmp without affecting the appearance of the picture?

(b) What will be the result of using that number of bits per pixel on the file size?

Comment

The answer is given at the end of this part.

We shall now try the above activity in practice and see what happens.

Activity 15 (exploratory)

With the file Reddish Vale.bmp open, go to 'Image' and then 'Decrease color depth'. You will see a dialogue box like that in Figure 25.

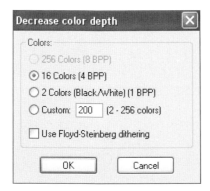

Figure 25 Decrease color depth dialogue box

Notice that the option '256 colours (8 BPP)' is not available. This is because the current colour depth is already 256. ('8 BPP' means '8 bits per pixel'.)

In the dialogue box, choose '2 Colors (Black/White) (1 BPP)'. Also, in the box next to 'Use Floyd–Steinberg dithering', remove the tick. (Dithering is a way of giving an illusion of there being more colours than there actually are, rather as grey can be suggested by juxtaposing small black and white dots. In all the following work we need this to be turned off.)

Watch the picture carefully as you click 'OK' to see if anything changes. You can choose Edit > Undo to revert to 256 colours, if you want to try again.

Do not save the file, as you will need to use the original version later. However, leave it with a colour depth of 2.

Comment

I saw no change when I switched between 256 colours and 2 colours, as expected.

Activity 16 (exploratory)

With the colour depth for Reddish Vale.bmp at 2 colours, look at the information pane. The 'Disk size' is still as before, because we have not changed the version of the file on the hard drive. (However, if we saved the file that is currently open, the version on the hard drive would be overwritten.)

What has happened to the 'Current memory size' (the size of the file in RAM)?

Comment

You should have found that 'Current memory size' has dropped markedly, to about 255 KB. It is now very close to one-eighth of the 'Disk size' (about 2 MB).

Do not save the changes you have made. There is no Close command in IrfanView, so Exit from IrfanView. (The Exit command is at the bottom of the File menu.)

We shall now look at the effect of decreasing the colour depth of Mellor.bmp in theory and practice.

Activity 17 (self-assessment)

Calculate 'Current memory size' for 16 colours, and put the value in the space in Table 2. I have not used MB to avoid confusion arising from the use of 2^{20} for 'mega' and 2^{10} for 'kilo' when referring to file or memory sizes.

Table 2 Data for Mellor.bmp with different colour depths

Image property	Current memory size
256 colours (8 bpp)	2 051 304 bytes
16 colours (4 bpp)	

Comment

The answer is given at the end of this part.

You will now use IrfanView to check the answer in the last activity.

Activity 18 (exploratory)

(a) Open the file Mellor.bmp with IrfanView. Decrease the colour depth to 16 colours and look for a change. You might well need to flip back and forwards between 16 and 256 colours to see any difference. The area where you are most likely to see a difference is in the sky, where there are some very light greys.

(b) With a colour depth of 16, is 'Current memory size' the same as was calculated in Activity 17?

Comment

(a) I found the difference between 256 colours and 16 colours very slight with this greyscale picture. (We shall see later what the effect is with a non-greyscale picture.)

(b) The current memory size of the 16-colour version is 1 025 224, which is not identical to the value calculated in the last activity, although the discrepancy is very small (around 0.04%). The answer is not exactly as predicted because not all the data in the file relates to the colour values of the pixels. This means that changes in the file size are not solely determined by changes in the number of pixels and colour depth.

Activity 19 (exploratory)

With Mellor.bmp open, decrease the colour depth from 16 colours (4 bits per pixel) to 2 colours (1 bit per pixel). The change should be instantly apparent.

Comment

You might have been surprised at how little black there was in the picture when you converted it to two colours. The amount of black is determined by the value of a threshold in IrfanView. Shades of grey that are lighter than the threshold are converted to white; shades of grey that are darker than the threshold are converted to black. In IrfanView you cannot adjust the white/black threshold, but other graphics editing packages do allow the user to adjust the threshold.

4.4 Compression

You learned about compression in Part 1 of this block. You should recall that there are two main types of compression: lossless and lossy. In lossless compression, the process of compressing and then uncompressing loses none of the information in the original file – hence the name 'lossless'. In lossy compression, on the other hand, information is lost irretrievably. When you converted *Mellor* to 16 colours and then 2 colours, you were in effect performing a type of lossy compression, because you lost information from the picture. The conversion of *Mellor* to 16 colours had a barely noticeable effect, so you might decide that the loss was worthwhile for the sake of the 50% reduction of file size it produced. The subsequent conversion to 2 colours was unlikely to be thought acceptable, even though it brought about a further significant reduction of file size. This demonstrates an essential idea of lossy compression, namely that a balance has to be struck between quality and file size.

You will try some practical examples of lossless and lossy compression now, starting with LZW compression. This is a lossless compression technique used in the 'zip' method of reducing file size.

Activity 20 (exploratory)

Open the file Reddish Vale.bmp. You are going to save this file in TIF format (TIF stands for Tagged Image File). The TIF format is a bitmap format, like the BMP format, but it allows lossless compression to be used during file creation.

Choose File > Save as. In the 'Save as type' dropdown box choose 'TIF – Tagged Image File Format'. You should now see something like Figure 26.

On the right, under 'TIFF save options' there are various compression methods you can choose. If you were to choose 'none', you would make very little difference to the file size. In terms of file size, there is little difference between BMP files and TIF files when used in their basic formats.

Choose LZW. Now look very carefully at the destination folder indicated in 'Save in' (at the top of the 'Save picture as' box). Your folder will be different from that shown in Figure 26. You will need to find this picture after you have saved it, so make sure you notice

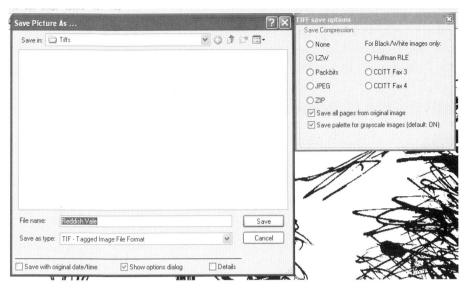

Figure 26 Saving file in TIF format with LZW compression

where it is saved to. You can choose a more convenient location if you want to by using the navigation facilities in this dialogue box.

Click on 'Save'.

To see what effect this has had, you need to go to the information pane and compare the 'Disk size' with the 'Current memory size'. However, the 'Disk size' data will not yet incorporate the change you have just made. To see the effect of the change, go to File > Open and open the TIF file you have just saved. Now go to the information pane and compare the 'Disk size' data and the 'Current memory size' data. Remember that the 'Disk size' is the compressed size, whereas the 'Current memory size' is the uncompressed size of the file in the computer's RAM.

Comment

You should have found that the 'Disk size' value was about 157 KB, a considerable reduction compared to the 'Current memory size' of about 2 MB. What this means is that the compressed file stored on the hard disk is about 8% of the size of the uncompressed file, which is currently in the computer's memory (that is, in the RAM).

As you will recall from Part 1 of Block 3, LZW compression works by looking for repeating patterns of coding, and creating a dictionary of shorter code words for the patterns. In the *Reddish Vale* picture there is a lot of repetition. For instance, because the only colours are black and white, every pixel has either the black or white value. All the white pixels are identically coded, and all the black pixels are identically coded, and there are many repeated patterns.

Activity 20 has applied lossless compression to a graphic which contained a lot of repetition. It achieved a significant reduction of file size. What happens when we apply this compression technique to *Mellor*, which does not have a lot of repeated data patterns?

Activity 21 (exploratory)

Use IrfanView to open Mellor.bmp. Save it as a TIF file with LZW compression as you did for *Reddish Vale*. Then reopen the file and check what reduction, if any, you have achieved.

Comment

When I did this I found that the file size increased! The 'Disk size' (the compressed size) was 2.05 MB, as opposed to the 'Current memory size' (uncompressed) of 1.96 MB. So this compression technique has actually increased the size of this file. With LZW compression, if the data does not consist of repeating patterns, not only is there no useful compression, but the creation of a dictionary increases the amount of data that has to be stored.

You can delete the file Mellor.tif as you will not need it again.

Files such as Mellor.bmp cannot be compressed significantly using lossless compression. Lossy compression comes into its own with files like these. We shall try lossy compression now on Mellor.bmp and Reddish Vale.bmp.

Activity 22 (exploratory)

Use IrfanView to open Mellor.bmp. Then go to File > Save as and in 'Save as type' choose 'JPG – JPEG Files', as shown in Figure 27. (Be careful not to select JP2 – JPEG2000. This is a development of JPEG, which, at the time of writing, has not become widely used.)

On the right, in 'JPEG/GIF save options' set the 'Save quality' slider to about 30. Note carefully the folder indicated in 'Save in:' as this is where your file will be saved. Choose a more convenient folder than the one shown if you wish, then click 'Save'.

Now use IrfanView to open the JPEG file you have just created. (You need to do this to update the information pane.) Then open the information pane and compare the data for both 'Disk size' (the compressed size) and 'Current memory size' (the uncompressed size).

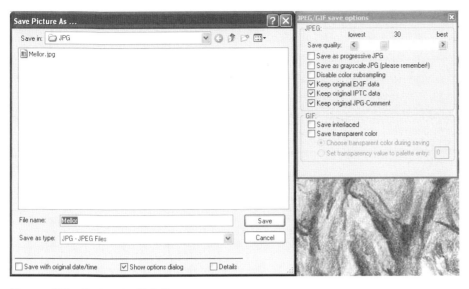

Figure 27 Saving in JPG format

Comment

When I did this the 'Disk size' had gone down to about 187 KB, indicating a very useful amount of compression, whereas the 'Current memory size' (the size of the uncompressed file) had shot up to nearly 6 MB.

The reason for the increase in size of the uncompressed file to around 6 MB is not hard to see if you look in the information pane at 'Current colors'. You will see that we are now using 24 bits per pixel, even though there are still only 256 distinct colours in this image. The JPEG standard is defined in terms of a colour depth of 24 bits per pixel, whereas the original BMP file used only 8 bits per pixel. The increase from 8 bits to 24 bits accounts for the approximately threefold increase in file size in RAM, even though there is not actually any more information in the file.

The lossy compression technique that worked so well with Mellor.bmp, with its many shades of grey, is not well suited to pictures such as Reddish Vale.bmp, which uses only two colours. You will confirm this in the next activity.

Activity 23 (exploratory)

Use IrfanView to open Reddish Vale.bmp and save it as a JPEG file with a quality of around 30. Then open the file you have created and look at the information pane. Compare the 'Disk size' (compressed size) and 'Current memory size' (uncompressed size). How much compression has been achieved?

Comment

I found that the size of the file on disk was about 346 KB, which is a fairly respectable reduction in file size. Bear in mind, however, that we achieved better compression using lossless compression of Reddish Vale.bmp. Using LZW compression we got the file down to 157 KB.

The JPEG process is not so much a single process as a family of compression techniques. You can think of the lossy part of the process as reducing some of the variations in the picture. When the variation has been reduced, there is more repetition, so lossless compression can be used to achieve further compression. There is therefore a built-in lossless stage after the lossy stage. The reduction in file size that we achieved in Activity 23, where we had a 2-colour image, is largely the result of the lossless part of the process.

What these activities have demonstrated, therefore, is that in images with few colours, and large expanses of identical pixels, lossless compression (for example, LZW compression) is effective. On the other hand, where the image consists of pixels with lots of different values, with little repetition, and with subtle variations between different pixel values (as in the varying shades of grey), lossless compression is often less effective than lossy compression.

4.5   From grey to colour

When I used the word 'colour' in the last section, I omitted the meaning that comes most naturally to most of us. In general speech, colour is the thing that a greyscale picture lacks. In everyday use, colour means redness, greenness, blueness, etc.

In computer graphics, the distinction between grey and colour (in the sense above) is a bit artificial. This is because greys are represented in the file and displayed in much the same way as reds, blues, greens and so on. In the last section when I spoke about pixels having a particular value (for instance, a value in the range 0 to 255), I was skating over several complexities. One of these is that the colour of a pixel on a display comes from combining three primary colours: red, green and blue. The next activity shows you how these primary colours can create other colours.

Activity 24 (exploratory)

Use the *T175 Colour demonstrator* software to look at the effect of combining red, green and blue. This opens on page 1. To change pages, click on one of the numbers 1 2 3 4 at the top right of the window. Follow the on-screen instructions.

Comment

The software showed you that mixing the three primary colours enabled you to create other colours. What it did not allow you to do was vary the brightness of each of the three primary colours. By varying the brightness of the primary colours and combining them appropriately, it is possible to create nearly all the colours we can see.

A computer display has millions of tiny emitters of primary-coloured light: some emit red, some emit blue and some emit green. Clusters of these emitters are grouped into pixels. The overall colour of the pixel is varied by adjusting voltages applied to the primary emitters within the pixel.

When you first open an image file in IrfanView, each pixel of the picture is displayed using one pixel on your screen. With the pictures we have so far looked at, there are more pixels in the picture than there are pixels in most computer monitors. What you are likely to see, therefore, is just part of the picture on your screen. If you zoom in or out, the relationship between pixels in the picture and pixels in the monitor changes. When you zoom out, a single pixel in the computer monitor represents several pixels in the picture. One way to do this is for the single pixel on the monitor to display the average value of the pixels it represents in the picture. On the other hand, if you zoom in so that the picture is magnified, a single pixel from the picture is spread across several neighbouring pixels in the screen. You will see an example of this shortly.

In a bitmap file, such as a BMP file or a TIF file, an 8-bit number is typically used to indicate the 'brightness' of a primary colour in a pixel. Because there are three primary colours, three 8-bit numbers are needed to specify all three primaries of a pixel. These three 8-bit numbers are run together to make a 24-bit number which represents the 'colour' of the pixel. For instance, here is a 24-bit binary number for the colour of a single pixel:

110010001100100011001000

Printed like that, it is not easy to interpret. It becomes slightly easier if we break it into three groups of 8 bits to reveal the amounts of the three primary colours:

11001000   11001000   11001000

(red)   (green)   (blue)

Each of these 8-bit binary numbers has an equivalent number in the ordinary number system that we use (the denary system). The denary equivalents are shown below, although you do not need to know how these are derived:

200   200   200

(red)   (green)   (blue)

Notice that, in this example, each of the primary colours has the same amount. In fact this pixel would appear to be grey. Grey results from mixing red, green and blue equally. Turning all three primaries off, by giving them a value of 0, 0, 0, produces black. When all three primaries have maximum values (255, 255, 255, in the case of 24-bit representation), the result is white.

Activity 25 (self-assessment)

Would the grey created by mixing red, green and blue with the values 200, 200, 200 be a dark grey or a light grey?

Comment

The answer is given at the end of this part.

Activity 26 (exploratory)

Use the *T175 Colour demonstrator* software, page 2, to look at some of the red, green and blue values for various colours. Follow the on-screen instructions. As you put the cursor over each patch of colour, its value is shown as a set of three numbers. These numbers represent respectively the red, green and blue values. Notice what happens with the greys. Check whether 200, 200, 200 is a light grey.

Comment

You should find that the greys have red, green and blue components which are equal. The light grey represented by 200, 200, 200 is an example.

Activity 27 (exploratory)

On page 3 of the *T175 Colour demonstrator* software you can adjust red, green and blue values independently in order to try to match one colour with another. Do not spend too long on this. It is intended just to show how colours change as you vary the amounts of red, green and blue.

Comment

I found it very difficult to match the colours. It wasn't straightforward to see how the primary colour components would affect the final colour.

You will now look in close-up at some pixels in a colour picture.

Activity 28 (exploratory)

Use IrfanView to open the file Loweswater.bmp and use the 'Plus' zoom button to zoom in as far as possible on the picture. (Alternatively, you can press 'Shift' and '+' on the keyboard to zoom in.) You will have to zoom many times until you reach the maximum. (If you have difficulties pressing the mouse button or keys so many times, just read my comment below.)

Comment

When you have reached the maximum, you will see that the picture is a mosaic of small squares. Within a square, the colour is the same, but from square to square the colour usually changes. These squares are the pixels of the picture. At this level of magnification, the pixels are quite big. Each pixel of the pictures is spread across many pixels of your computer screen.

With 24 bits per pixel we can have 256 different red values, 256 different green values and 256 different blue values. This means that the total number of colours that can be displayed by a pixel is:

$$256 \times 256 \times 256 = 16\ 777\ 216$$

A monitor that can display this number of colours is sometimes said to be showing 'true colour'. It is supposed to correspond roughly to the number of colours the eye can distinguish. In fact, it is hard to specify precisely how many colours the eye can distinguish because so much depends on the individual and the viewing conditions.

Activity 29 (exploratory)

Zoom out again until your screen is showing all the *Loweswater* picture. (You can zoom out either by clicking on the minus icon, or just by pressing the minus key on your keyboard, or you could just reopen the picture instead.)

Now, on the menu, go to Image > Decrease Color Depth. You will probably find that '256 Colors' is already selected. (Select '256 Colors' if it is not already selected.) This is showing you how many there will be if you click 'OK', not the current colour depth.

Click 'OK' to reduce the colour depth to 256 colours, and watch for changes. You will see the changes most clearly in the sky where it changes from blue to white over the hills. (Go to Edit > Undo on the menu if you want to try this again.) If the effect is not clear, make sure that in the 'Decrease Color Depth' dialogue box there is no tick next to 'Use Floyd–Steinberg Dithering'.

Now reduce the colour depth to 16 colours.

Comment

The effect of the reduction to 16 colours is particularly marked in the lake, where banding of colours should be quite clear.

It is quite usual for digital cameras to provide 'true colour' pictures. However, given that digital-camera pictures (at the time of writing) typically have 3 or 4 million pixels, and that in 'true colour' each pixel is represented by 3 bytes (24 bits), a single uncompressed photograph would be in the region of 9 to 12 MB. At the time of writing, a memory card for a digital camera typically has a capacity of 128 MB, and would therefore hold only about 10 pictures. The large size (in memory terms) of these pictures is what makes the use of JPEG compression virtually standard with digital cameras.

The JPEG process works by taking blocks of pixels in the picture and analysing how the colour changes across each block. The data in the JPEG file records the patterns of variation across groups of pixels, not individual red, green and blue values for each pixel. When the picture is viewed, however, these patterns of variation have to be translated back to individual red, green and blue values.

Compression in JPEG files is achieved by reducing the variability of colour in places where the reduction is unlikely to be noticed. The technique exploits that fact that the eye–brain combination is relatively insensitive to changes of colour. You can get a sense of the eye's insensitivity to colour change from the following activity.

Activity 30 (exploratory)

In the *T175 Colour demonstrator* software go to page 4 and follow the on-screen instructions. The software demonstrates that quite large changes of red, green or blue values are quite often imperceptible.

Comment

When I did this, I started with yellow. I could not see any difference between the left and right sides of the square until I added 48 units of blue. With green I needed about 60 units of red. In other words, I was unable to notice quite large changes of colour.

One of the by-products of JPEG compression is the introduction of artefacts (some feature that was not in the original) into the picture. These are most noticeable at low quality settings.

Activity 31 (exploratory)

Use IrfanView to open Snowdrop.bmp. Save the file in JPG format with a quality setting of 5. Then open the file you have just saved.

Comment

You should readily see a degradation of image quality. Some of the detail has been lost.

In practice, such a low quality setting as 5 for a JPEG image would be unlikely to be used. But what sort of quality setting would be more reasonable? The answer largely depends on what the image is for, and at what scale it will be viewed. Unfortunately IrfanView does not make comparison of images easy, so I have assembled into one image a number of versions of the *Snowdrop* picture at different quality settings.

Activity 32 (exploratory)

Open the file Snowdrop Comparison.bmp. The top left version has not had any lossy compression applied. The remaining versions have been saved as JPEG files at the quality settings shown, and then pasted into this composite image. Try zooming in a few steps when you look at each image.

Comment

To begin with, along the second row, you might be hard pressed to see any difference between the pictures and the original, and between the pictures themselves. However, by zooming in you should have been able to see differences.

Lossy compression techniques, such as JPEG, sacrifice subtle variations of colour in order to reduce file size. But for lossy compression to work successfully, there must be subtle variations to sacrifice. You might recall that with the picture *Reddish Vale* the JPEG process was not so impressive. In that picture there were no subtle variations of colour to sacrifice: every pixel was either black or white.

4.6   Other formats

IrfanView allows you to save files in a number of other formats. Two of the most widely used of these other formats are GIF and PNG. Both of these are intended primarily for use with Web graphics (for instance, on websites). The GIF format incorporates LZW lossless compression. It also restricts files to a colour depth of 256 colours (8 bits per pixel). Thus, if you start with a file with more than 256 colours and save it as a GIF, it will have only 256 colours after you have saved it.

Activity 33 (exploratory)

In IrfanView, open the file Lakeside.bmp. Look at the information pane, and check the 'Number of unique colours', which should be many more than 256. Then go to File > Save as and choose GIF – Compuserve GIF. (Do not be misled by the quality slider. It does not apply when saving in GIF format.) Save the file in GIF format.

Now open the GIF file you have created (Lakeside.gif) and look at the information pane. You should see the 'Number of unique colors' is 256. Look at the lake, where the banding of colours should be very clear.

Comment

The GIF format was devised at a time when the number of viewable colours on the Web was quite restricted, hence the use of only 256 colours.

The PNG format (Portable Network Graphics) is also intended primarily for use on the Web. It incorporates lossless compression, but is not restricted to 256 colours.

Activity 34 (exploratory)

In IrfanView, open the file Lakeside.bmp. Go to File > Save as and choose PNG – Portable Network Graphics. You will see that you can set various compression levels.

(a) Set the compression level to its maximum, and save the file. Check its compressed size.

(b) Reduce the colour depth to 256 colours and save again in PNG format. Check the compressed size (i.e. disk size). How does it compare with the GIF version of the same picture?

Comment

(a) I found the size of the file was about 1.4 MB, which was about half the uncompressed size.

(b) I found the compressed size was about 304 KB, which was slightly smaller than the GIF file (330 KB).

Because GIF and PNG files use lossless rather than lossy compression, you might think that they would have limited usefulness as formats for graphics on the Web. However, graphics created for the Web (icons, symbols, buttons, etc.) often use relatively few colours, and the data in them is often repetitive – perhaps because there is a prevailing colour in the design. These factors make them well suited to lossless compression, unlike, for instance, photographs of natural scenes.

Finally, you might like to look at how your computer is set up to show images. Activity 35 does this.

Activity 35 (exploratory)

You can see some of your computer's display settings by going to the Windows 'Start' button, and then choosing Settings and then Control Panel. Depending on your version of Windows, you should choose either 'Display' or 'Appearance and Themes' and then 'Display'. When you get the 'Display' box, choose the 'Settings' tab. You should then see how many colours your monitor can display, and how many pixels it has.

Comment

When I did this, I saw the display shown in Figure 28. You will have seen something similar, but it is unlikely to have been identical.

Figure 28 Display settings for a computer

Figure 28 shows that my computer is set up to show 1024 pixels horizontally and 768 vertically. It is also set up for a 32-bit colour depth.

You may have spotted that 32 bits cannot be split equally between red, green and blue. In fact 32-bit colour is usually 24-bit colour, but with an additional 8 bits allocated for further information not directly related to colour.

In these activities we have not explored many of the other things that IrfanView can do. You can learn a great deal more about graphics and graphical editing simply by exploring the functions of the menu buttons and looking at the results – both on the screen and in the information pane. If you have the time to spare, you might like to do this. However, for the purposes of this course you do not need to go any further than you have done in these activities.

5 Computers and animation

This section consists of a short movie *Computers and animation* that you will find on the course DVD. It is best watched just before or after studying Part 1, Section 5.

This movie, split into six sections, describes the way that computers and computer software have transformed the way that animations are created and used by the entertainment industry. Today, computer generated imagery (CGI) is used extensively to provide virtual sets, animated scenes and characters in movies, TV programmes and adverts. Full-length CGI movies featuring animated characters – to which audiences relate almost as they do to human actors – are huge box-office successes. Animated characters and special effects now integrate so well with 'real' life as to pass almost unnoticed.

Using commercially available CGI software, the six sections of the *Computers and animation* movie illustrate the way that CGI software is used to create virtual sets, objects and actors and animate them and then combine them with actual movie sequences.

In the introduction, the movie gives examples of animations and introduces 'Edna' the animated cockroach, who plays the starring role in a spoof advert for the fictional 'StainX' detergent.

StainX was developed as promotional material by the software house that produced the CGI software.

Section 1 then introduces the deformable mesh – the basic CGI structure – from which backgrounds and objects are constructed as 3D models within CGI programs.

Section 2 looks at the way that attributes of 3D models – particularly colour, texture and lighting – are used to add realism to scenes and objects.

Section 3 describes how 'simple' CGI objects such as sharks, spaceships and cameras are animated to move within scenes.

Section 4 shows how digital puppets are animated to move and behave realistically.

In Section 5 we see the way that digital puppet actors like Edna and her friends and family are integrated with actual movie footage to create the finished visuals.

Finally, Section 6 presents the entire *StainX* movie starring Edna the cockroach, including the audio track.

Activity 36 (exploratory)

While you are watching this DVD session, make brief notes on each part. Afterwards, review your notes (perhaps in conjunction with reading the audio script) and organise them in a logical fashion.

Comment

When I did this, I noted several things I felt were important including the use of meshes, templates, masks, key frames and interpolation to produce the 'simple' animation of objects such as the spaceship and the more complex animation of articulated digital puppets such as Edna. I was impressed by the use of camera and lighting effects in CGI and the way that everything can be combined so well with real video material. Your notes will probably cover a wider range and in much greater detail than my brief outline.

ANSWERS TO SELF-ASSESSMENT ACTIVITIES

Activity 4

You should obtain a display like the following. You can resize the chart by clicking on it and then dragging on a corner.

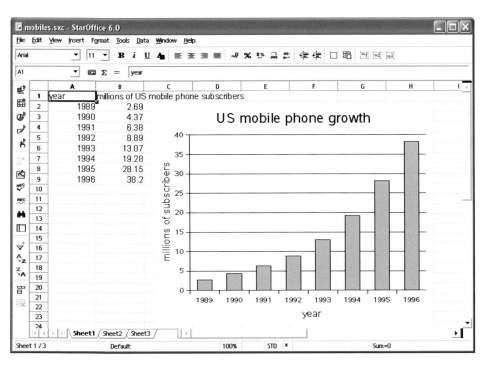

Figure 29   Spreadsheet display with column graph of US mobile phone growth

Activity 9

The plot using a logarithmic scale shows that the growth is *not* exponential – in fact, it is *slower* than exponential, since the increment in column heights gets less as the square size increases, as shown in Figure 30.

Activity 10

In both cases the growth is roughly exponential, as can be seen from plots on a log scale. Exponential growth is quite common during the early years when a new technology is being adopted, although such growth cannot go on for ever!

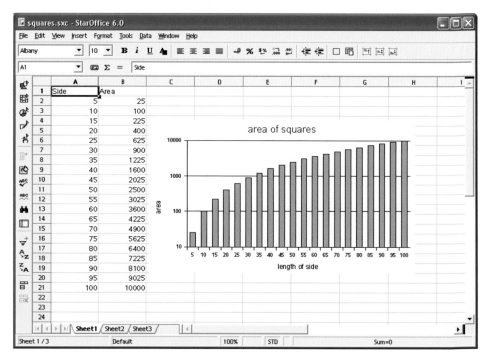

Figure 30 Spreadsheet display with column graph of area of squares

Activity 14

(a) One bit per pixel will suffice. This is because we need to represent only two colours: black or white. We could use 0 to represent black and 1 to represent white.

(b) The file size will be reduced considerably if we use 1 bit per pixel. There will still be about 2 million pixels, but each one will be represented by 1 bit rather than 8 bits. We can expect the file size to shrink to one-eighth of its former value.

Activity 17

Going from 8 bits per pixel to 4 bits per pixel means halving the number of bits per pixel. This halves the file size, so the answer is 1 025 652.

Activity 25

The 200, 200, 200 grey is much closer to 255, 255, 255 (white) than to 0, 0, 0 (black), so it would be a light grey.

REFERENCE

Taylor, E. V. (2004) 'Real news meets IT', [online] T175,
The Open University.

ACKNOWLEDGEMENT

Figures 21 *and* 22 – Artist E. Allan Jones, used by kind permission of Dorothy Jones.